# SIR, I REPRESENT . . . .

## or,
## Christian Salesmanship

by

William E. Cox

**BAKER BOOK HOUSE**
Grand Rapids, Michigan

# CONTENTS

# THE AUTHOR

William E. "Ed" Cox was born in Charleston, West Virginia, in 1923. He attended Alderson-Broaddus College, West Virginia Institute of Technology, and Morris Harvey College, from which he received his B.A. In 1958 he earned the B.D. degree from Eastern Baptist Theological Seminary in Philadelphia, Pennsylvania.

Ed has been in sales work for well over twenty years. His first selling job was as a newsboy while still attending grade school. Other sales experience includes door-to-door selling, route selling, and factory representative. In the capacity of sales manager he has hired, trained, and taught salesmen.

Mr. Cox is also an ordained minister, having been ordained by the West Virginia Baptist Convention in 1947. He is the author of six theological books, as well as smaller pamphlets and articles. Cox has been active in youth and social work. For two years he was an institutional chaplain at Greatersford Prison near Philadelphia. During World War II he served for three years in the 80th Tank Battalion, 8th Armored Division—one of the fighting units in the famed Battle of the Bulge.

At present he lives in Vienna, Virginia, with his wife, Osa, and their son, Timmy. Twin sons are serving in the Air Force, and a married daughter lives in Charlotte, North Carolina. Cox is co-owner and president of Vienna Typesetting Service, Inc.

# INTRODUCTION

The ideas in this book have been hammered out on the anvil of personal sales experience. The writer has had over twenty years of experience in the field of selling. It follows naturally that many ideas have been read and heard along the way from many thousands of successful salesmen. It would be almost impossible to recall the source from which each idea or statement has been borrowed. However, in order to keep plagiarism at a minimum, sources will be acknowledged whenever they can be recalled.

There are no panaceas in this book for the order-taker. It is a book for salesmen, or for those who want to become salesmen. Most sales "pitches" are put together with fragments from the repertory of those who have blazed the trail before. I have tried, however, to dress the ideas in this book in new garments.

Who among us has not had the sale slip through his fingers simply because he failed to apply properly his knowledge of selling? Or because some tool had not been sharpened lately? This book will review some of the tools of selling, and will place them in their proper order. This will serve as a primer for those who are just entering the thrilling field of selling and, I trust, will also be a good refresher course for those who are past masters. It should enable any conscientious reader to close more sales. Interested?

*Blessed is the man who has some congenial work, some occupation in which he can put his heart, and which affords a complete outlet to all the forces there are in him.*
—John Burroughs

# I ABOUT SELLING

Voltaire once said: "If you wish to converse with me, define your terms." Since there are differing schools of thought as to what constitutes good selling, let us first define our terms. What do we mean when we speak of selling? Here is my definition: *Selling is the performance of a service which meets a definite need in the life or business of a customer.* Any transaction not fitting this description is not worthy of the name selling.

Goods may be transferred from one location to another, companies may make profits, and salesmen may draw commissions, but unless you have met a need on the part of the customer—you have not practiced the art of selling. It is an obvious fact that millions of people daily exchange much money for items they do not need. This is done through the use of mass media advertising, gimmicks, unethical canned speeches, and so forth. But does this destroy our definition of selling? It merely points up the need for this book!

The fact has been emphasized, in our definition, that a genuine sale meets a definite need on the part of the customer. *Ninety percent of your prospects will not realize that they have a need for your product unless you make them aware of it.* It is that fact which separates the salesman from the order-taker. A salesman will show the customer his need while the order-taker will wait for him to stumble over it.

A sale will not even begin to take shape until you cause the prospective buyer to be honestly dissatisfied with his lot without your product. In order to sell a person, you must draw such a mental picture in that person's mind that he values what you are selling more than he values the amount of money required to purchase the product. Once he is completely convinced that your product will enhance either him, or his family, or his business—or all three—then he is ready to buy; you have sold him.

Please note that we are talking now about convincing the customer of his *legitimate need*. This has nothing to do with fast-talking him, or of maneuvering against his best interests. According to Alexander Pope: "A man convinced against his will, is of the same opinion still." Let every salesman take note!

A satisfied customer will thank you for having shown him his need. This is what makes selling such a rewarding profession. This is what makes repeat sales. Let me illustrate my point. I was calling on the purchasing agent of one of the largest and best known chemical plants in America. "Mr. Cox," he said, "we appreciate, more than we can tell you, having factory representatives call on our people; for each one of you is a specialist in his own field." "And," he continued, "you keep us abreast of ideas and changes which we would otherwise not know about. We have estimated that our factory representatives [salesmen] increase our profits by several thousands of dollars each year. Thank you again for calling on us."

This is why selling which meets a need brings satisfaction to the customer, to the salesman, and to the company for which he works. This type of selling will result in a minimum of closed doors on the next call. And in a minimum

8

of returned merchandise, warm letters to the company, and the like.

## PRACTICING THE GOLDEN RULE

This is a good place to make the point—if indeed I have not already made it—that the Golden Rule still works. Yes, it works especially well in selling. I pity the man who carries his religion in one compartment and his job in another. If this be preaching, then it is preaching unashamed!

The Golden Rule does not make one any less a salesman. One can practice it and still show the customer his need, i.e., sell him. If you were the customer (and each one of us is at some time or other) and were not aware of a need, you would want someone to show you. Is not this the Golden Rule in practice? "Do unto others as you would have others do unto you."

Although Jesus made the Golden Rule live by living it himself, he was not the only person—in fact, he was not even the first—to advocate this philosophy. Confucius, who lived 500 years before Christ, said: "What you do not wish done to yourself, do not do to others." Emerson was paraphrasing the Golden Rule when he said: "The only way to have a friend is to be a friend."

An example of the Golden Rule at work in our twentieth century is found in the alleged actions of a baseball hero. I am thinking of Willie Mays, the great star outfielder of the San Francisco Giants. Willie is said to have signed a contract without even reading it or discussing price. When asked about this, Willie replied: "I came here to play baseball; these gentlemen will pay me what I am worth."

Willie's latest contract was signed guaranteeing him $100,000 per year!

Marshall Field & Company instructs its salespeople: "One of the most important factors in successful selling is getting the other person's point of view; we believe that if a salesperson actually tries to put himself in the customer's shoes, he can't go too far wrong in his selling attitude." What is this except practicing the Golden Rule in selling?

\* \* \*

The Golden Rule can also be made to work in reverse order. I read of an insurance adjustor who offered a motorist a few dollars to have a bumper straightened. The motorist thought he deserved a new bumper, which would cost ten times the amount offered to straighten the old one.

"How about this," the motorist suggested, "let me ram your bumper and bend it, and I'll pay you the same amount you are offering me. Will you make this a deal?"

He got his new bumper.

The Golden Rule causes us to do what we must do anyway if we would make repeat sales. For example, about two out of five customers who quit trading at the average store, quit because they feel salespeople are indifferent to them. I can best illustrate this point by relating a personal experience.

I went into town looking for a particular style of dress shoe. I saw the style I wanted, only to learn the store did not have it in my size. The shoe salesman attempted to sell me a different (though similar) style *in the wrong size.* I called his attention to the size, but he insisted it was the correct size for me. Then—after he saw he was losing the sale—he admitted that the shoe was too small for me, took my name and telephone number, and volunteered to call me as soon as my style and size came in.

Result? I went across the street and bought a pair of shoes. Though they were not the style I had desired, they were at least the correct size. Had this salesman reversed his tactics, i.e., had he *first* offered to get my size and style of shoe, then call me, he would no doubt have had a sale plus a repeat customer. As it turned out, he lost both.

To carry the point further—suppose for a moment that the shoe salesman had been "successful" in getting me to take the tight-fitting shoes home. Every time I wore them—assuming I did not return them to his manager and demand a refund—I would have vowed never to return to that store.

Even though he might have rung up the price, wrapped the shoes, and sent them from his store to my home, that young man would not actually have *sold* anything. For he would not have met a need. My need was not for an undersized pair of shoes!

\* \* \*

There is all the difference in the world between a *filling* station and a *service* station. Most of us recall the headiness and indifference which came over so many gas station owners during the war—when gasoline was so scarce that they could easily move their entire allotment! It was amazing how many former service stations suddenly became mere filling stations. Many station attendants became arrogant as they realized they were no longer bound by the laws of supply and demand. Courtesy went out the window, and in some stations it was difficult even to have one's windshield cleaned.

Once the war had ended and gas again became plentiful, motorists by the thousands began bypassing the filling stations in order to patronize the service stations. Oil companies are trying desperately to change the image in people's minds. Literally thousands of stations have closed their doors or changed hands several times. · To ignore the Golden Rule in one's selling is to court disaster.

No salesman who practices the Golden Rule is going to be indifferent to the needs of the customer. After all, wouldn't the salesman like for the other person to be friendly? "Do unto others as you would have others do unto you." "Good will," said Marshall Field, "is the one and only asset that competition cannot undersell or destroy."

A word of caution may be in order here. Let the Golden Rule be a natural part of your selling. The customer will sense it the instant you fake it. Don't underestimate his intelligence.

Speech teachers tell us that a good outline is so well prepared it hides itself as the speaker moves smoothly from one point to the next. Our Golden Rule customer service should be built into our presentation so smoothly—and so naturally—that it hides itself from being conspicuous. It should become a natural part of our relationship with each customer.

\* \* \*

The art of selling, we conclude, goes beyond the moving of goods. It goes even beyond making money. Genuine selling is customer-centered; it meets a need for the customer.

*If you would like to leave footprints in the sands of time, you had better wear work shoes.*

—Survey Bulletin

## II ABOUT THE SALESMAN

To define selling is, at the same instant, to define a salesman. *A salesman is one who makes his living by performing a service which in turn meets a need in the life or business of another.* Not a brilliant statement, this, yet what a pregnant one! For this amounts to more than a definition; it is a biography.

Are you a salesman? How do you line up with the above definition? Could you improve upon your present image? It is well for every person in the selling profession to take stock of himself occasionally.

It is important for a salesman to appreciate his occupation. Selling, like every other field, has been stereotyped. In the minds of some people, all salesmen are fast-talking, deceptive, sleight-of-hand artists. Some unthinking people have the attitude of "Oh here comes another 'salesman.'" These people treat all salesmen with contempt.

This attitude has caused some salesmen to become self-conscious and somewhat timid about calling on the trade. No person who permits himself to be influenced by such stereotyping can do his best work. Nor is the type a true portrait of a good salesman. On the contrary, the salesman can hold his head high—knowing that he is a member of the very fibre of his nation. It is a true saying that "nothing happens until someone sells something." Robert S. Fogarty, Jr., director of personnel for the furniture division of Daystrom, Inc., remarked: "Each salesman has over

100 company employees dependent upon him for their very existence. I know of no challenge—no responsibility—which exceeds those incumbent upon the man who sells."

Every field has its unscrupulous counterfeits. However, we do not attach the name "shyster" to every member of the legal profession just because there happen to be shyster lawyers. We do not call for the impeachment of every congressman simply because some members of Congress take bribes, or perjure themselves, or are proved to be sex perverts. Then why should any person be ashamed of being a salesman simply because of the minority who bring discredit upon themselves while posing as salesmen?

Then, if you would put your best foot forward as you practice self-expression, throw back those shoulders (not far enough to make you seem arrogant!) and let there be a smile of satisfaction on your face. Let there be a light spring in your step as you leave home each morning, repeating to yourself: "*I* am a salesman; I belong to one of the world's finest professions." For, after all, if you are truly a *salesman* then you can sincerely make this boast. Selling, according to *Fortune* Magazine, is "the biggest man-made force to keep the American economy going." In 1952 there were some 4 million full-time salesmen in the United States. Selling is one of the largest occupational groups in the world. We could paraphrase Lincoln's statement about the poor man and say the Lord must love salesmen or he wouldn't have made so many of them.

Selling as a profession is relatively young. In bygone days editors used such terms as "public nuisances" and "preying vultures" to describe salesmen. However—and let us not forget this—these terms were used during the very infancy of selling. They certainly are not applicable today in referring to the entire range of salesmen. A small minority indeed would meet this description today.

* * *

The following quotation caused me to square my shoulders and to take increased pride in the art of selling.

### PORTRAIT OF A SALESMAN

Just the other day we received a letter full of questions from a lad named Billy. Though it was sandwiched in among thousands we receive here at the *Post*, it stopped us because it contained a particularly thought-provoking query. Billy asked: "What is a salesman?"

In these days of priorities and business-as-unusual, Billy's question seems particularly pertinent. Here is our answer to Billy . . . our portrait of a salesman.

What is a salesman? He's a lot of things, Billy. He's a front office buck private . . . a general in the field.

He's the fellow that feeds a thousand stomachs every day in the year—stomachs that belong to those who make and distribute the things he sells. But he seldom finds time to feed his own face at home with Mom and the kids.

He's a credit department, pack horse, reporter, host, story teller, technician, display man, and it's a hundred to one bet, he's a grinning dyspeptic—but grinning, mind you, Billy.

He knows how to say yes when he'd like to say no. And he can say no when yes would be easier.

While politicians wrangle, while dictators play cops and robbers, while dreamers dream—the salesman's the bird who's showing the world a constructive brand of fighting . . . fighting that will preserve the American way of living. He's out there selling. Whether it be chewing gum or tractors, he sells—sells those things that make Americans American.

17

Quotas to him are sales convention handicaps that make the game fun. Others may work a forty-hour week. But the salesman kicks because there are not more hours in every day. He's the fellow that does while others don't. And he loves it!

That's what a salesman is, Billy.

Let's hope he keeps on being himself—for the sake of the life we enjoy in the U.S.A.

—The Saturday Evening Post

## SOME TRAITS OF A GOOD SALESMAN

### He Never Quits School

A good salesman never quits school! By this I mean that the successful salesman is ever evaluating himself both as a person and as a salesmaker. He is ever learning, ever improving.

Large companies and corporations invest thousands of dollars annually in ascertaining which personal characteristics result in bigger and better sales. An examination of their findings should prove profitable to every salesman. What traits are shared in common by outstanding salesmen?

Robert S. Wilson of the Goodyear Tire and Rubber Company made a survey of 150 purchasing agents, asking them to "think specifically of the best salesmen representing any company who call on you, and tell us briefly why you consider them best." The majority of the purchasing agents did not place technical knowledge first. It was the man himself and how he fitted into the total situation. The report abounded in such adjectives as "considerate," "dependable," "friendly," "honest," "sincere."

18

Surveys carried out by other companies placed the following general qualifications high on the list.

1. A liking for people.
2. A love of selling (sales drive).
3. Aggressiveness with people but not too much.
4. Average or better emotional control.
5. Steadiness—staying power.
6. Industriousness; not needing to be pushed.
7. Getting along with fellow workers.
8. Loyalty to the firm.
9. Ambition and self-improvement.
10. Freedom from impulsiveness.
11. Strong motives to keep working.

According to another survey, good salesmen are: self-starters, extroverts, moderately dominant, self-confident, good social mixers. They know their products well, are keen observers and investigators, sound analysts, and good strategists.

How are you measuring up so far? See any room for improvements? It is helpful, on occasion, to sit down and just have a candid talk with oneself. Imagine that you are on the other side of the purchasing agent's desk. Look at yourself as you appear to him. Would I want me (or a carbon copy) to walk into my office? And would I buy, repeatedly, from such a person—if I were the buyer? This can prove to be an eye-opener. Try it once in awhile.

**He Practices Auto-communication**
There is a verse of Scripture which teaches: "As a man thinketh in his heart, so is he." One good result of our conversations with ourselves might well be that we come away with an improved image of ourselves—perhaps, after

a few alterations following the self-interview. Psychologists speak of auto-communication, and say this is one of the surest roads to self-confidence. Auto-communication has to do with a person telling himself what he is, and doing it so convincingly that he begins to live the part. A sales bulletin from our home office told of a successful business man who at one time worked as a salesman for our company. According to the bulletin, "Pony" had two enemies to overcome—an inferiority complex and a stuttering habit. "All I did," Pony said, "was to begin looking on myself as a champion. I don't know where the idea came from, but the minute I began looking on myself as a champion salesman, I began to become one." Pony was practicing auto-communication. Or—to go back to the source—"As a man thinketh in his heart, so is he." Try it. It works.

### He Is a Good Listener

One very important trait in most top salesmen is the art of being a good listener. This is not a trait with which the average salesman is born. Rather, he must work hard to acquire it. For, true to the nature of the breed, salesmen like to talk. After all, they make their living by using words. Therefore, there is a temptation for the salesman to forget to listen. And yet there is a wealth of information to be gained from the thoughts of the customer. How else can we learn of his likes, dislikes, needs, and so forth?

The salesman needs to listen, not only to the customer, but he needs to listen, occasionally, to other salesmen, to his company, to his wife, and even to his competitors! Gold is where you find it. Listen, then, for needs, clues, dissatisfactions, leads. Listening to the customer puts him where he rightfully belongs—in the center of the picture.

### He Has Sales Drive

Psychological studies have shown that a love of selling, or "sales drive," is essential for sales success. Even though selling is one of the best paying professions in the world, those who enter the field merely to make money will usually fail. To be successful in the best sense of the word, a salesman must gain psychological rewards along with the monetary dividends.

### He Is Himself

A salesman should, by all means, be himself at all times. Most of us have seen persons who endeavored to imitate another person. To do this is to court disaster and ridicule. Recall the minister who mimicked his favorite seminary professor. That which was quite natural to the professor is as out of place as two left feet to the imitator. Or recall the pet words which run throughout some sales organizations. Perhaps the word is nothing more profound than "golly" or "gosh." But practically every person in that organization uses the pet phrase. Don't you imagine many a purchasing agent has enjoyed a chuckle after the salesman has brought along his boss, and the buyer has noticed that the two sound like Siamese twins? Be yourself! Be your best self. Be your very best self. But be yourself.

### He Uses His Tools

Any good craftsman uses his tools. This should be especially true of the salesman. Most companies furnish, at no extra cost to the salesman, literature, specifications, and many other sales tools. The smart salesman will let these tools work for him. He knows that they are the result of the accumulated experiences of many who have blazed the trail ahead of him. The Chinese proverb has it that one picture is worth ten thousand words. Our selling tools enable us to draw a more descriptive picture of our product. It is said by some psychologists that we learn eight times as much through the sense of sight as through any of the other senses.

### He Takes Refresher Courses

Another good practice for the alert salesman to follow is the habit of giving himself a refresher course occasionally. We have said that the successful salesman never quits school. All of us recall vividly the "intellectual inventories" of our school days. These tests served to show both pupil and teacher where extra help was needed in a given subject. A review of our sales materials can serve this same role. It is possible for the best of us to get in a rut in our presentations. It is much like adding a column of figures incorrectly. Often we will make the same mistake each time we go over them. A backward glance at some of our sales-helps might be very profitable in pointing up some common mistake we may have fallen into. We may even be misrepresenting our product! Finding this mistake can sharpen our pitch and put added commissions into our pockets, while assuring the customer of better service.

### He Competes Primarily Against Himself

Most experienced salesmen have learned the secret of competing directly with themselves, while competing only indirectly with other salesmen. Let me explain. By competing directly only with yourself, you will automatically improve your own latent abilities. This a person can do without feeling threatened. In competing with others, on the other hand, one is likely to become frustrated, owing to the fact that the other person might have natural capabilities to which you could never measure up. Modern educators are becoming increasingly aware of this fact. More and more they are insisting that one student should not be pitted against another student, but that each student should be challenged merely to do the very best of which he is capable.

I once knew a horse which had not learned that competing with others was futile. I learned about this weakness in Dusty the hard way. We were riding one Saturday afternoon with an experienced rider who was mounted upon a sleek race horse, while I was astride Dusty. Frank spurred his horse, and before I knew it I was holding on to Dusty for sheer life. For Dusty, you see, had a philosophy that no other horse—regardless of size or ability—should ever be allowed to get ahead of him. Well, the race horse could just naturally outdistance Dusty; and this was nothing for a horse as small as Dusty to be ashamed of. However, Dusty was not content just to compete against his better self—he was determined that even a race horse should not outrun him. By the time Frank finally realized what was happening and reined in the race horse, Dusty had run in the cindered path behind the race horse until he was all but blinded, his body was covered with dust and cinders, and he was on the verge of bursting his heart. He finally ran up a bank and into a fence in sheer desperation, trying to outdistance a horse which by natural inheritance was far his superior.

Some salesmen, unfortunately, have not learned the lesson Dusty needs to learn. Consequently, they go out day after day and literally knock themselves out trying to outdistance some other salesman whom they have seen work.

These men would be much better off to recognize their own very best capabilities and then work within the limits of those talents. Actually, they would realize more sales by working relaxed than by trying to go beyond their limitations.

I am reminded here of the salesman whose boss kept saying to him: "Get those calls up." So the salesman went beyond what even the boss expected of him. For one day his boss asked him if he had got in more calls the past week. "Yes sir," replied the salesman, "I got in seventy calls last week; and I could have gotten in more, but some smart-alec asked me what I was selling."

### He Toots His Own Horn—But Gently

Success carries with it accomplishments. Therefore, all successful salesmen have whereof to boast. And it doesn't hurt to toot your own horn—with reservations. Someone has said: "It's not enough to live right; you've got to let people know you live right." So, accentuate your positive traits. Let your customers know when you win an award. They like to do business with a successful person. Just be careful not to inject too much vitamin "I" into your conversations.


## SOME PITFALLS TO AVOID

The things covered in this chapter thus far have been, for the most part, dealt with from a positive viewpoint. Now, at the risk of running counter to the "power of positive thinking," let us wax negative for a while. Let us look at some "don'ts" for the salesman—some things he should avoid doing.

24

The salesman should never let his limitations overcome him. Like Dusty, the horse, we all have our limitations. If we are short, we can never be tall; if we are bald, we can never expect to be called "Curly," except in a joking manner. Our limitations, if they truly are that, should be recognized as such and made the best of. This goes back to self-acceptance.

Some of the world's greatest people have succeeded in spite of (sometimes on account of) their disabilities. There once lived an English statesman who had lost both his legs and spent the rest of his life on crutches. One day this statesman gave a command to a subordinate The subordinate countered that what his superior asked was an impossible task. "Young man," said the statesman, "I walk around on impossibilities every day!" The order was carried out.

Few persons would have blamed Franklin D. Roosevelt had he given up his ambitions in 1921. For it was in that year that he was stricken by the dreaded crippler, polio. Mr. Roosevelt said that his hardest task after that was to move one toe! Yet, in 1928 this determined man was elected Governor of the state of New York; and later became the first and only man in history to be elected to four terms as President of the United States.

Many pages would be required to mention the many names of the great persons in history who became great in spite of seemingly insurmountable handicaps. If these greats could be called in to speak to salesmen, all would echo one central message: don't be overcome by your limitations; consecrate them, and let them work for you. Helen Keller said: "I thank God for my handicaps, for, through them, I have found myself, my work, and my God." Such an attitude would be beneficial to any salesman.

Aristotle has said: "The ideal man bears the accidents of life with dignity and grace, making the best of the circumstances." This brings to mind the story of a salesman who practiced Aristotle's dictum, in selling. The salesmanager sent a salesman to sell shoes in Borneo, where the natives went barefoot. The salesman wired back that there was absolutely no market for shoes on the island and that he requested an immediate transfer. Then a second salesman was sent to the same island. His cablegram read: "Send twenty gross immediately; nobody here has em." The first salesman in this story gave up in the face of difficulty, while the other salesman consecrated his difficulties, making them work for him.

### Avoid Overselling

Any salesman is liable to fall into the habit of overselling. I have actually seen salesmen talk themselves out of the sale after the customer had said yes. A salesman, like any other speaker, should stand up, speak up, and then shut up. In every presentation there is a psychological time to close. We run a great risk whenever we talk beyond this point. Someone has said: "If you can sell by saying 'ba,' then don't say 'ba ba.'"

### Avoid Making a Bad Exit

I believe it was while I was in the Army that I read the article which brings this point to mind. The only thing I recall about the article is that it cautioned the reader to shine the backs of his shoes as well as the toes. The point being made was that people watch us exit as well as enter. This is good advice to the salesman. We never know when we are selling. An ungracious or flippant departure may well squelch our chances of any future orders. So, make your exit as good as your entrance. It will pave the way for your future calls.

### Avoid Taking the Spotlight

Too much vitamin "I" will kill any sale. A good selling atmosphere is one in which the customer occupies the center of attention. After all, you are there to ascertain *his* need, and to meet *his* need. We already have mentioned that salesmen like to talk. This being so, there is a danger that we might talk about the wrong persons—ourselves! "I think," "I want," "I would like to send you . . . ." The customer is not interested in what *you* think, or want. He is interested in what you can do for *him* or for his business.

### Avoid Waving a Red Flag

A salesman's job is to motivate the customer into a buying mood. There is an old axiom that you can't antagonize a person and sell him at the same time. So, don't bring up touchy subjects. Certain words just naturally antagonize certain people; these should be carefully avoided. Avoid such words as: "sell," "c.o.d.," "sign here," "you need," and other such red-flag words. Instead of "I have to ship you c.o.d."—you might say: "Mr. Jones, just pay the driver when he brings the merchandise." You have conveyed the message, yet without the offensive word. Select your words carefully. They are your best selling tools.

### Avoid High Pressure

High-pressure salesmanship is, by common consent, the worst type of all. Products having real merit require no such tactics. Obviously, high-pressure salesmanship may be self-defeating. Such a salesman can easily insult the friendship of the offended merchant.

### Avoid False Claims

Never promise more than you can deliver, or more than your product will do. It is always thrilling to walk in, after a sale, and have the customer say: "Sam, your product did all you said it would and much more." This builds repeat business. However, a sure way to lose business is to make a false, or exaggerated claim for your product. Customers will long remember the letdown which often comes during their greatest need for performance. Unless you are absolutely certain that your product will meet the stated needs of the customer, it is wise to admit your ignorance at this point. Some salesmen find that it makes a good impression on their customer to invite him to try the product whenever they, themselves, are uncertain. Let's say, for example, that your customer asks you whether or not your product will do a certain job in his business. A good reply might be: "By golly, Mr. Jones, you have asked me a hard one; I'm not sure that I can give you an intelligent answer. So suppose we try it out together." Most customers will appreciate your honesty as well as your interest in their problem.

* * *

Experience proves that it is more difficult to unlearn a bad habit than to learn a good one. Therefore, every salesman should take personal inventory occasionally. He should seek to unlearn any bad habits formed over the years, and, at the same time, be ever striving to improve himself as a good salesman.

*. . . Most people like to work—when a favorable work atmosphere is present . . . .*
                                    —Industrial Management Bulletin

# III  ABOUT THE COMPANY

"Sir, I represent . . . ." These words—or similar ones—have begun many a conversation leading up to a sale. Around these words careers have been launched, factories have been built, nations have grown. From the time Christopher Columbus' sailors bartered with the Indians, America has been a nation built around salesmen and the companies they represent.

What, exactly, is a company? One dictionary defines it as an association of people to carry on a business. The salesman is very much a part of the company; he represents the company. In many cases, the salesman is the only person from the company who actually comes in contact with the customer.

Every company has personality. This personality is made up of every member of the organization. To do his best, a salesman must represent a company which has a good personality. It would be difficult, if not impossible, for a salesman to practice the Golden Rule for long if his company were unethical. This presents a real challenge to the reputable salesman. He must make certain that the company of which he is such an integral part is one that he can represent unashamedly.

Selling, even at its very best, tends to be a lonely business. A salesman must be a self-starter, and he also must be willing to be "on his own." For his marching orders take

him to the farthest outpost on the territory. It is, therefore, essential that the salesman feel that his company
stands behind him, and is with him in spirit, though not
in bodily presence.

The company, for its part, owes it to the salesman to
furnish him with the very best of tools available, to keep
the lines of communication open at all times. It owes
it to him to recognize the importance of the part he plays
in the organization, and to let him feel that his contribu-
tion to the company is an important one. Nothing wilts
the collar of the hard-working salesman quite so much as
being taken for granted. He will respond to a sincere
compliment more quickly than to a matter-of-fact bonus.

It behooves every company to take stock occasionally and
to make sure that the men in the front lines are properly
equipped. Many companies have gone bankrupt because
they failed to see, in time, that communications had broken
down between the front office and the sales force. Salesmen—and this is presupposing that they are good ones—
are the heartbeat of any company. Each company should
beware lest the arteries leading to its heart become clogged
by indifference, lack of understanding, unanswered com-
plaints, and the like.

Although the following illustration does not relate to
salesmen, it is, nevertheless, apropos in showing the relationship between morale and production.

The United States Steel Company had tried, unsuccess-
fully, to improve employee understanding and efficiency.
There seemed to be a point below which accident rates
could not be cut. The company posted authoritative rules
on its bulletin boards. Violators of thes instructions were
sent home for a day. Still, accidents persisted. Finally,
the company's leadership decided upon a revolutionary

plan—a new, "psychological" approach. Employees were called in in small groups for their suggestions on how their particular operation could be made safer. These sessions were held in clean conference rooms amidst a relaxed atmosphere. Coffee was served. It was an exciting experience as the men argued and exchanged ideas. For the first time these men were seeing that they were important members of the company team; that their advice was important; and that they could help improve the safety of their own operation.

This new approach to safety was called "Operation Attitude," and was first introduced in United States Steel's Chicago plant. That plant had had the highest accident rate of any of the company's main plants: 2.29 accidents per million man-hours. Within two years, that rate had been cut to a sensational low of .66, the best in the company's history.

This company learned that wherever employees were consulted about their jobs, morale generally rose, and so did production.

Many companies could increase sales tremendously by putting into effect an "Operation Sales Attitude," similar to the one mentioned above. Much sales potential goes begging because of discontent in the field. And—keeping in mind that the better salesmen have a reputation for griping—I am speaking here of legitimate grievances which could be remedied by concerned company officials.

Top management may sometimes become so engrossed in the overall business that the salesmen are treated as expendable pawns on the chessboard. In showing a profit or meeting a payroll the company may well jeopardize its future sales if it ignores the feelings of its sales force. Most companies spend much money for advertising; but every company should beware of building one image in the public's eye while its own sales force is left with a completely different image. This type of advertising borders on false economy.

It is a grave error for any company to feel that all it needs to supply its salesmen with is money. This is to slander the intelligence of the salesman. If *esprit de corps* is to prevail, incentives offered the sales force must certainly be broader than mere monetary rewards.

Sociologist Richard Centers said, after sampling national attitudes: "If non-reward should become more universally the citizens' lot than it is now, we can only expect disillusion and radicalism to become more prevalent." We might add that disillusioned radicals will not long do their best jobs of selling.

Revolutionary changes have taken place in our society in recent decades. Companies need to be cognizant of these changes. We have advanced far beyond the point where men labored merely for food, shelter, and clothing. The term, "business conscience," is used today when American Big Business is scrutinized. Progressive companies today are finding that increased production results from coffee breaks, restful color schemes, et cetera. Not too many years ago this sort of thoughtfulness toward the employee would have been unheard of. Today it is standard operating procedure.

Companies do well to furnish each salesman with a job analysis along with his job requirements. Simple though it may sound, this small routine will do much to head off bewilderment as well as infraction of company rules. Every salesman needs to know what is expected of him; he also needs to know the boundaries of his territory and the boundaries of his authority. An ounce of prevention in this direction is worth many pounds of cure. For many salesmen have done irreparable damage because of lack of knowledge of company policy. And, more often than not, these mistakes have stemmed from hazy instructions— or no instructions at all.

In drawing up job classifications, the company must be careful not to stereotype its salesmen. Each salesman is an individualist; this is, in fact, what makes him a good salesman. If he worked well in a mold, he would be on an assembly line rather than bucking the rigors of selling. One of the surest ways to kill a salesman's incentive is to stereotype him.

While companies are treating their salesmen as individuals, it is important that each territory be studied in its own light. Very few territories are exactly alike. Even the Buying Power Index (if it stands alone) is not an adequate guide in every case. Sections of the United States vary in their product preferences and buying habits. Many elusive factors enter in, such as race, creed, ethnic origin, types of industry, income brackets, climate, etc., ad infinitum. Some communities suffer economic reverses almost overnight. The loss of a government contract can make the difference between prosperity and pauperism in many communities. So can the closing of mines. Inequities in quotas may result if a company fails to consider each territory separately.

A salesman welcomes goals. However, these goals must be attainable when his best efforts are put forth. Some company officials, unfortunately, work on the theory that if they ask the impossible, they will in this way get every ounce of production that their sales force is capable of producing. This theory has been exploded many times over. When confronted too often with such goals, salesmen are more likely to shrug their shoulders and become passive. "Why put forth the effort?" they will reason, "I never seem to satisfy company demands anyway."

## SALES MANAGERS

The salesman's closest contact with his company is through his manager. Companies extend themselves through their sales managers. Where the company is large enough, there will be different echelons of management. A company errs sadly whenever it chooses these managers on the basis of friendship (or kinship) rather than ability. For salesmen resent being supervised by inferior managers. Every salesman wants a manager whom he can present to his customers with pride, and one to whom he can look for needed guidance. This does not come from a manager who became a boss through popularity with the company rather than on his own ability. Furthermore, salesmen prefer managers who are more than supersalesmen.

According to numerous typical surveys, good salesmen resent it when their company takes a supersalesman and elevates him to a mere pusher. For this is all such a manager can be. Salesmen want a man to whom they can look for knowledge, help, and understanding. This does not result when the only claims a manager has to fame are his past sales record, and perhaps a back-slapping personality. Few men are inspired to do their best for such a manager as this.

On the other hand, a good manager—one who couples his salesmanship with integrity, common sense, friendliness, the ability to listen sincerely—can infuse new life and vitality into just about any sales organization. Companies owe it to their salesmen, and to themselves, to seek out such men for promotion.

A manager many times can either make or break a salesman. A good manager will develop the best that lies within a salesman and even bring out latent talents that perhaps the salesman himself did not realize he possessed. The salesman's pride—or lack of it—in his company will come primarily from his manager.

\* \* \*

Few companies enjoy a seller's market in today's changing, selective society. Success will be short-lived for any business organization that ignores the customer. And good salesmen are too much in demand to be taken for granted very long. Therefore, it behooves each company to examine occasionally its management as well as its relationship with each customer and each member of its own sales force.

*The customer is not a cold statistic—he is a flesh-and-blood human being with feelings and emotions like your own, with prejudices and biases . . . .*
—Beneficial Management Corporation

# IV  ABOUT THE CUSTOMER

A basic element in any sales situation is the customer. The more the salesman knows about his customer, the more likely he is to close repeat sales. If the company could not get along without its salesmen, certainly the salesmen could not long exist without the customer. What can be learned about the average customer? Although each person is an individual, all people have certain traits which are held in common.

The customer is part of a moving society. Since World War II, twenty percent of all Americans have changed their place of residence at least once every five years. Part of this moving is owing to necessity, while another part of it shows the restlessness and adventurous spirit of those people who are your customers.

Our customers belong to an informed society. We not only live in the midst of a population explosion—we are also witnessing an explosion of knowledge. It is estimated that the quantity of information about virtually every subject is doubling every ten years. This information is being disseminated through our mass communications media almost as quickly as it is discovered; indeed, sometimes it is passed on as it happens. This presents a genuine challenge for the salesman to keep abreast of all that is happening, so that he can converse intelligently with his customers.

We stated earlier that selling meets a need on the part of the customer. Here, we need to elucidate on the meaning of "need." Needs differ from one person to the next. One person may need to bolster his ego, while another may feel perfectly fulfilled in his social standing; this second person will buy your product only if it meets a pragmatic need, while the customer suffering from an inferiority complex may buy to meet a psychological need. Others buy merely to satisfy a whim. Tests have shown that customers frequenting department stores will sometimes pay extra to get the color they want. For example, towels which were identical in size, name brand, and texture, differing in color only, were stacked side by side. A much higher price tag was placed on one particular color than was put on any of the other stacks of towels. Customers actually looked at all stacks, then purchased the higher-priced towel because it was the color they liked.

Therefore, to say that some customers buy what they need while others buy what they want is to describe two sides of one coin. For, psychologically, a desire stems from a deep-seated need. It may be a need for prestige, for attention, or for some other psychological longing. This explains why middle-class people often change their wardrobes to conform with the prevailing style while wealthy people are likely to wear the old, comfortable garments; the wealthy do not need to prove their positions by their dress! Our rule (that selling meets a need) still applies, whether the need be physical or psychological.

Fifty years ago, selling was based on supply and demand. Today, it is geared to "what's on the customer's mind." It is no longer enough to ask what he wants, but what style, size, color, odor, and so forth. Millions of dollars are spent annually on marketing research and motivation research to ascertain these facts, thus anticipating customer demand. This science is still in its infancy, and there are still many unknown quantities. For, in spite of the herd instinct, each customer remains an individualist.

As an individualist, the customer resents being stereotyped. This is why canned sales pitches enjoy only a limited success. They are geared to only a limited number of people. Successful public speakers have learned to evaluate their audiences before writing their speeches. They know that the same speech will not please every audience. Every salesman plays the role of public speaker each working day. Though he usually speaks to an audience of one, it is equally important for him to evaluate every audience before planning his presentation.

Today's customer is accustomed to service and convenience. Supermarkets have long since learned the secret of placing "impulse items" within easy reach of the customer. Drug stores have undergone amazing changes even in our generation. I can still remember when the drug store specialized in prescriptions and patent medicines. The customer knew that the druggist had a few other items such as toothpaste and shoe laces, but these were kept out of sight in a drawer. Today, these—along with hundreds of other items—line the counters and gondolas, at the fingertip of the customer. Yes, the customer is accustomed to service and convenience—and he *expects* both.

Your customer is a veteran at listening to sales pitches; in 1959, it was estimated that the average American was subjected to 1,518 sales messages a day. This number no doubt has increased by now. So, your pitch had better be sincere and honest. Your customer will wait to be sold. Another thing could be said about these pitches—most of them are done by professionals via the radio, TV, magazine, or newspaper. The customer is therefore accustomed to a personable salesman; and he will expect the same from you. Dudley J. Taw, vice-president of McKesson and Robbins, Inc., says: "What is the big reason for sales success? People! . . . Customers today are shopping for nice people to do business with." There is no substitute for service and friendliness.

Your customer is a member of a society made up of upper, middle, and lower classes. Sociologists seem generally to agree that there are five distinguishable classes in America—two upper classes and three supporting classes. The two upper classes are made up of managers and professional people, while the supporting classes would be composed of the blue-collar worker along with the skilled, semi-skilled, and even the unemployable. A reading of Vance Packard's book, *The Status Seekers*, will point up to what extremes these classes are pushed. The salesman who practices Golden Rule selling must guard against exploiting these class distinctions in order to make a sale.

Regardless of the type of selling you are in, many of your customers will be women. Women have gained a new prominence in the nation's economy. More women are working than ever before. They have entered fields heretofore reserved for men. Along with the job-holding, they play a great part in handling and spending the money. Many purchasing agents are women. It has been estimated that men earn 80 percent of the family income, while the women spend 85 percent of it on consumer goods and services. Women also own 65 percent of the nation's savings accounts, 74 percent of titles to homes, and 65 percent of the private wealth.

* * *

Strive to know all that you can about customers, both collectively and individually. Train yourself as a student of human behavior. This will enhance your customer relations immensely. Learn all that you can about your individual customers. Valuable sources of information are the local newspapers, radio, and television stations. Perhaps some of your customers have entered or even won a style show, or horse show, or chess tournament. Any such information will give you clues as to some of their tastes and sense of values.

*Know thy work and do it.*
—Thomas Carlyle

# V  ABOUT THE SALE

Now that we know what selling is; what makes a salesman; something about our company; and something about the customer—let's get out in the field and actually make a sale. We'll run through the sale all the way from the pre-approach to the close.  We shall also deal with what I shall call the post-approach.

## THE PRE-APPROACH

Every call should be planned in advance, not later than the night before the actual call is made.  With pencil and paper in hand, the salesman should think through every call he plans to make the following day.  A little planning before the call can keep the proverbial foot out of the mouth during the call itself.  Know all that you can about the customer. What are his likes and dislikes? How should I best approach him?  What did I leave hanging on my last call which might be a natural place to begin this call? Has my customer been in the news lately?  Or a member of his company or his family?  A sincerely placed compliment might be just the thing to lead to a buying mood.

What are the needs of my customers (individually)? Treat each customer as an individual—never as part of the herd, or as a clay pigeon you are to knock down in order to "make a sale."  He will sense it if you take him for granted, or stereotype him.

What objections am I likely to encounter on each call? How could I sincerely overcome these objections? And am I going out to sell, or merely to take orders? Selling and order taking, remember, are as different as chalk and cheese.

How could I best get each customer involved? Few sales, if any, result from a monologue; genuine sales are the result of dialogue. Plan to get the customer involved in the sales situation. Don't leave this to chance; work it out during your pre-approach.

What tools or samples will I need for tomorrow's calls? Have everything planned so that you will have what you need, at your fingertips, on every call. If the customer has asked you for information, have this information assembled and take it with you when making the call.

Hugh Chalmers once said: "Salesmanship is nothing more nor less than making the other fellow feel as you do about the thing you have to sell." Decide, before calling on the customer, just how you feel about the particular items you plan to sell him. How can you best make him feel the same way about them?

Most of what we have said thus far on the pre-approach applies to buyers whom the salesman already knows. However, planning before the call should also be done on "cold-turkey" accounts as well. Never face a buyer without some pre-planned objectives. Once in a great while your objective may be nothing more than to gain information as to the customer's need. Even on these calls, plan ahead as to a minimum of things you want to learn from this customer; other questions will come to mind during the interview. The more you can find out about the customer and his needs before the interview, however, the more likely you are to close on the first call. Comparatively few lasting sales are ever made without carefully laid plans.

We have said that selling meets a need on the part of the customer. In many cases, the salesman will need to make the customer aware of his need before selling him. For many of your customers will not realize that the need exists until you show them; after all, their minds are on many things. Here, too, your strategy for doing this should be mapped out before you get face to face with the customer.

## THE SALE ITSELF

Our planning has been done to the best of our ability; our sales kit is in good order; we have all the samples, estimates, diagrams, and information we need for the day's calls. Now we are ready to begin making those calls and writing those orders. We plan to start early, knowing that the hours from eight to twelve noon will either make or break our day. Let us run through the sale, step by step.

### Qualify the Buyer

The first order of business on the call itself is to qualify the buyer, i.e., make certain we are talking to the man who actually can sign the order for this particular product. Many hours have been wasted in talking to the wrong party! Unless you have called on the buyer before, a good approach is to go to the receptionist and ask, "Who does the buying of bearings?" Once she has referred you to a party, make doubly sure before beginning your pitch. "Mr.

47

Jones, I understand you do the buying of bearings; is that correct?" Then introduce yourself and sell him.

## Put Your Best Foot Forward—Every Time

The old adage about familiarity breeding contempt should always be kept in mind by the salesman as he enters the office or shop of the prospective customer. Untold numbers of buyers have changed their source of supply for no other reason than, "Joe took it for granted that he had this account sewed up, so I decided to teach him a lesson."

So, as we begin our calls today, let's remember to approach every customer with an air of respect and as a challenge to our salesmanship. A number of salesmen have shaken his hand since you made your last call; and a great many circulars have crossed his desk. New products are constantly coming on the market. Even if we have some customers in our pocket, just remember that competition is trying to pick our pocket.

## Control the Interview

It is very important that the salesman control the interview, keeping the customer on the subject at hand. Keep the customer in the center of the picture, but be sure that it is a sales portrait—not a rehash of golfing or of current events. Let him talk, but see that he talks about your product or his need for the product. This requires finesse, but it is absolutely necessary if your day is to be profitable for all concerned. There will be times when the customer has time on his hands, and he may just want to ramble. You must be a good listener, but you must be ready to steer him back on course whenever he goes too far afield.

Since you have planned the interview—he probably has not—lead the customer. Suggest not only that he buy, but

48

*what* he should buy and how much. Actually, this saves him time. If your presentation is a logical one, he will thank you for guiding his thinking. He expects you to know your products, e.g., their sizes, weights, packaging, and the like.

In guiding the interview, you will want to give the customer some choices. However, those choices should not include the choice to buy or not to buy. When you present the order for his signature, never offer him the chance of saying "yes," or "no." Guide the interview in such a manner that his final choice will be "either-or" rather than between yes and no. "Mr. Prospect, would you prefer delivery on the tenth or on the fifteenth?" Or, "Mr. Customer, do you prefer this in the white or the blue?"

**Create the Need for Your Product**
Keep in mind that, while selling meets a need, your buyer may or may not be aware of his need. During the course of the interview you must bring about a dissatisfaction with his status quo. So long as he is happy with his lot, he is not likely to purchase. As you create the need you must guard against being offensive. You dare not reflect on his taste or lack of it. Yet, you must paint a picture in his mind of what his circumstances could be with the addition of your product. Your methods of doing this will vary from one customer to the next. You might use questions, or suggestions, or pictures to show how other customers—in his same line of business where possible—have arrived at a better position than his by using your product. Whatever method you choose, you will want to do three things: (1) fix a problem; (2) make him dissatisfied with his present situation in relation to the problem; (3) offer a solution to his problem.

### Demonstrate the Product

Nothing sells like a demonstration of the superior features of a good product. The demonstration shows the customer what the product will do. During a demonstration, we will let the customer handle the product long enough to become attached to it; then we will take it from him, and this will cause him to desire to have it back. There is a psychology of possession involved in this gesture. Having once handled the item, the customer has formed an attachment to it.

During the demonstration you will want to show as many uses for the product as possible. For, after all, the more uses he can put it to, the more likely the customer is to buy an article. And *showing* him these uses is far better than *telling* him. Let him suggest possible uses, too. If he mentions a specific problem—and if you can solve that problem with your product—you have just about assured yourself of a sale. So, demonstrate your products.

### Answer His Objections

An ounce of prevention, remember, is worth a pound of cure. Therefore, anticipate as many of his objections as possible; and answer these during your presentations—before he has a chance to voice them. You anticipated as many of his objections as possible during your pre-approach. You also planned ways to answer these by the demonstration. Each objection is a minor roadblock between you and the sale; the sooner these roadblocks have been cleared away, the sooner you can hit the target.

During the presentation itself, you will want to be listening for objections which you may not have anticipated. These are bound to come; so smoke them out into the open, where you can get at them. Then meet them head-on.

Objections, usually, are a call for help on the part of the prospect; he is simply asking for further information. He is saying: "Convince me that I should go ahead and buy this article from you." Someone has suggested that the objection is the prospect's last line of defense.

A keen salesman will turn objections into sales. Each objection will indicate to the salesman what points he needs to clarify before the sale is completed. If the customer were not interested he would, in most cases, simply have said no. But he hasn't said no. He has put forth an objection, which indicates that he is definitely interested. His objections should be treated as pleas for help. He is saying: "Show me how I can work your product into my budget"; or, "Help me to justify buying this item." Never let an objection discourage you; it is an excellent barometer.

### Ask for the Order

The more often you can ask for the order, without antagonizing the customer, the more likely you are to get it. After all, this person knows why you are there; he *expects* you to ask for an order. Some salesmen I have known made good appearances, good pre-approaches, and good presentations—only to balk at the most essential thing of all, i.e., they froze when it came time to ask for the prospect's signature on the order.

One salesmanager dramatized his point about asking for the order. At the beginning of the sales meeting he placed an expensive object on the table before him. "One thing I want to emphasize during this meeting," said the salesmanager, "is that you should always ask for the order." In a few minutes, he made another similar remark. About that time a sharp-thinking salesman in the room interrupted the salesmanager and asked if he might have the item on the table. The manager tossed him the gift and said: "You were the first salesman to ask for it; so, it is yours."

A request for the order is simply an attempt to close the sale. A good salesman will close early and often. A trial close is much like a trial balloon; it will bring forth an objection if the customer is not quite ready. This helps the salesman to determine whether or not he is taking the right approach with this particular customer. Each attempted close will elicit some sort of response. These responses convey messages to the alert salesman. They let him know what the customer is thinking.

There are psychological times to close a sale. A good salesman will learn to watch for these openings. A close should be attempted following each affirmative nod of the customer's head; following each question as to packaging, price, and so forth; and especially following each time you have satisfied his inquiry about a specific need your product will meet. In other words, close when he is ready. Close *whenever* he is ready. Use questions as check points to see whether he is ready to buy. Try often; but always leave the door open. Ask for that order. Keep reserve closes handy, but fire your trial balloons at every opening.

Someone has well said, "The secret of the signature on the dotted line is not a flying wedge or an easy wedge; it's the result of a planned sales presentation that 'closes' every step of the way." Someone else has called the close the five "heres." . . . (1) here is what it is; (2) here is what it will do; (3) here is the way it comes packed; (4) here is the way we deliver; (5) here is the amount I suggest.

**Take Along a Booster**

Astronauts know the worth of boosters in getting rockets into orbit. Without them, the nose cone would fall to the ground without ever having left the earth's atmosphere. Many sales have fallen short for want of a booster or two.

In this simile of rockets and boosters we are thinking of the main planned sales approach as the rocket. Our rocket boosters are planned extras which we can offer the customer if the need arises. Such extras as a contract price, for example, give the customers our ten-case price but agree to ship and bill the merchandise five cases at a time. Another booster might be in the form of dispensers or racks for the product. Still another extra (booster) might be some sort of extra service relating to our product.

Oftentimes—when the boosters are not needed to launch the sale—these extras can be thrown in after the sale itself has been closed. This is a wonderful way to build good will.

A smart salesman spends much time on the planning board before sending his rocket (sale) to the launching pad. And he would never think of firing the rocket without boosters held in ready reserve. A couple of good boosters may save him the time and effort of going back to the drawing board.

**Make Necessary Alterations**

Every salesman knows that his customer's needs (and tastes) are subject to change. Sometimes these changes can be sudden. Plan as you will, you may find that once you get into the interview your approach to this particular customer must change if you are to meet his need. Perhaps his need changed since your last call. Or perhaps there are problems related to his available space, budget, demands, etc., which you could not possibly know about until the interview was under way.

Remember that this customer is an individual. Though one hundred other persons might be delighted with what you are suggesting to him, your sincerest planning may run counter to *his* tastes. He may have a phobia (most of us do). It could be that certain odors, or colors, or textures are just simply offensive to this particular buyer. This will usually show in his reaction to your proposal.

Now this is not a suggestion that the salesman change his presentation every time he encounters a negative response. Many times the customer will need to be made aware of his need for the items you suggest. Even though your suggestion runs counter to his *personal* tastes, it may be the only type of product that his company can use.

Be alert for indications that you are "playing in the wrong key." Then, "think on your feet," and make quick modifications in your presentation. After all, why are you in this buyer's office? Aren't you there to meet *his* need?

### Take the Shortest Route to the Sale

The preceding nine points are steps to a sale. However, these steps should be our servant—never our master. I would say that in most cases you will climb these stairs to a sale. And, usually, you will climb the stairs more or less in the order of their arrangement. However, there will be cases where you can climb these stairs two steps (sometimes more) at at time.

You may be talking to a sharp purchasing agent who can follow you up the stairs at an accelerated pace. Never feel that you have to spend an allotted time on each step.

Some buyers might be two steps further up, wondering when you will come on up. Such cases might be compared to an amusing story I once heard. It seems that the congregation was joining the minister in reading the Twenty-third Psalm responsively. One lady was lagging behind in the reading. Finally the minister interrupted the responsive reading with this comment: "The rest of us will now pause beside the still waters, until one dear lady gets out of the green pastures!"

Don't take unwarranted shortcuts. Build your case, and make certain the customer is with you on each step before moving to the next one. But do watch for those refreshing cases where you can dash up the stairs barely touching—or even skipping—some of the steps leading to the sale. Some customers will already be aware of their need for your product when you walk in. They may even have been looking for just such an item. Such a customer's first question or response may let you know that you can close the sale. Here would be one of the cases where it would be foolish to say "ba ba." One "ba" would be sufficient here.

## SELLING INTANGIBLES

For the sake of clarity, our steps to the sale have presupposed that we were selling tangible items. However, these same steps—except the demonstration—apply equally well to the salesman who handles insurance, or stocks and bonds, or other intangibles.

The seller of intangibles must be especially thorough in one of the steps to the sale. This step is the pre-approach. In order to create a need for *his* product he must know something of the prospect's family, personal ambitions, tastes, and so forth. The insurance salesmen who make the "Million Dollar Round Table" have, without exception, made a long, painstaking study of these things with reference to their clients. And such is the case with *every* successful seller of intangibles.

The seller of intangibles must call on the added skill of converting his demonstrations into word pictures. His samples are limited to data concerning his service. He cannot play upon the senses of taste and smell. But all the other senses are at his disposal; and the lack of these two senses is compensated for by the fact that he deals with the future happinesss of the client or the client's family. True, he must play out his tune on fewer strings, but his melody is close to the heart of the customer.

## THE POST-APPROACH

A good post-approach will enable you to do a smoother follow-up on the customer involved. It will also lead to finesse on your calls in general.

Following each interview—preferably with a signed order in hand—rethink the interview. Have a curbstone conference with yourself. What did I do wrong? At what points did I lose control of the interview? Do I need more product knowledge before calling back on this account? Or a better working knowledge of his business? Did I oversell him? If so, why?

Some would prefer holding the post-approach at the end of the working day—thus leaving the salesman's mind free between calls to be sharpening up his planning for the next call of the day. *Whenever* the curbstone conference is held, it should by all means take place, not later than the end of the day. After all, the salesman has dollars and cents riding on his ability to profit from his mistakes and his ability to improve as a salesman.

Three things might be suggested concerning the post-approach: (1) be frank with yourself; see your mistakes and plan to do something about them; (2) learn from these mistakes; (3) then *forget them*—by this I mean that the salesman should not use precious time worrying over something that has already happened and cannot be recalled. I like the old Chinese proverb: "You can't change the past, but you can ruin the present by worrying about the future."

\* \* \*

Every genuine sale results in numerous benefits. These benefits are enjoyed by the customer, the salesman, and the company. Selling, you will recall, meets a need in the life or business of the customer. Granted, he may not recognize this need until he is faced with a well-prepared sales presentation. Each step to the sale (from the pre-approach through the post-approach) is vitally necessary to a good presentation. Strive to improve your use of each of these steps; then a higher percentage of your daily calls should result in signed orders.

*Every generation enjoys the use of a vast hoard bequeathed to it by antiquity, and transmits that hoard, augmented by fresh acquisitions, to future ages.*

—Thomas Macaulay

## VI  ABOUT OUR SALES PHILOSOPHY

This chapter is added somewhat as an appendix to the
rest of the book.  Since every salesman is a product of
his heredity and environment—and since every salesman
forms a personal philosophy as a result of his background
and experiences—perhaps we need to sharpen up our phi-
losophies, along with all our other sales tools.  This would
square with what we said earlier about there being a time
when every salesman should just simply listen to others in
order to learn from them.  Let us listen now while the
philosophers speak to us salesmen.

> *Make the best use of what is in your power, and take the*
> *rest as it happens.*                                    **—Epictetus**

It has been well said that there are three watchwords for
the happiness hunter—self-recognition, self-direction, and
self-expression.  To these one might add self-acceptance.

Self-recognition will cause a person to see his good points
as well as his weaknesses.  Having recognized his weaker
traits, he is in a good position to begin a program of re-
direction. Re-direction will automatically result in a better
self-expression.  The wise person will accept himself, but
will continually strive for self-improvement.  He will practice the dictum of Admiral Thomas C. Hart, who said:
"Dear God, give us strength to accept with serenity the

things that cannot be changed. Give us courage to change the things that can and should be changed. And give us wisdom to distinguish one from the other."

*Things are in the saddle and ride mankind.*
—**Emerson**

Selling, we have said, is among the highest paid professions in the world. The salesman works hard, and—as the apostle Paul teaches—a laborer is worthy of his hire. However, a salesman who makes money his only goal in life cannot possibly practice the Golden Rule. Nor can he be happy.

Money can serve as a good means to an end, but it always disappoints whenever it becomes an end in itself. Money is one of the poorest of gods! All who worship at its shrine come away empty and depressed. Pity the salesman whose only incentive for selling is to make money. And beware the company that holds out the making of money as the paramount motivation to its sales force.

What we have just said about money can be applied to "things" in general. Material things alone can never bring happiness to either the salesman or his family. It was Francois de La Rochefoucauld who said, "Before we set our hearts too much on anything, let us examine how happy they are who already possess it." How many people have you ever known, or read about, who were made happy by mere money or prestige alone? Some of the loneliest people in the world are those whose only goal in life is to make money—or to gain status just for the sake of status. I can think now of people known personally by me who have two things in common with each other: (1) Each has an abundance of material possessions, e.g., two cars, swimming pools, beautifully decorated homes, and all the

60

other Madison Avenue signs of "success"; (2) each has a nervous stomach, and devotes more space in his suitcase to pills than is devoted to clothing! This is living? This is success? These are the main rewards of selling? A thousand times "no!"

Certainly this is not a wholesale condemnation of making money. And I am in no way opposed to the acquiring of the luxuries which only money can buy. I am simply saying that the tail must not be permitted to wag the dog. We must put first things first. Paul did not say that *money* is the root of all evil. Rather, he said that the *love* of money is the root of all evil.

Thomas Carlyle's essay on "Labor" comes to mind just here. Said he: "A man must get happiness out of his work. That's the first of his problems: to find the work he is meant to do in this world. Without work he enjoys, he can never know what happiness is. Blessed is he who has found his work; let him ask no other blessedness. He has a work, a life-purpose; he has found it, and will follow it . . . . Labor is life." With this philosophy towards his selling career, the salesman is on the road to happiness. Money, and "things" will follow as a natural by-product. But these will not be, as Emerson termed it, "in the saddle."

*Lost: Somewhere between sunrise and sunset, two golden hours, each set with sixty diamond minutes. No reward is offered, for they are gone forever.*
**—Horace Mann**

Few people in the world need to be guardians of their time as does the salesman. For time truly is his most important investment in his work. I take issue with those who go so far as to say that time is the salesman's *only* asset. Every

**61**

good salesman has an abundance of assets other than time. However, the emphasis is a good one. Arnold Bennett's *How To Live on Twenty-Four Hours a Day* should be required reading for every salesman.

*It's but little good you'll do watering last year's crop.*
—*George Eliot*

The tallest fish stories are built around the ones that got away. And perhaps you have heard the one about the conversation between two salesmen. First salesman: "Boy, I really lined up some good leads yesterday." Second salesman: "Yeah, I didn't make any sales either."

Salesmen can't build success today on the big ones that got away. Or even on past good experiences. On the other hand, it is unwise for a salesman to become discouraged if he finds that his past performances were below par. Rest assured that none of us has done his best at all times. Mary Pickford once said, "There is always another chance . . . . This thing that we call 'failure' is not the falling down, but the *staying* down."

Every salesman can improve himself by putting forth the effort. Even seasoned men who look back on years of successful selling could improve. They could profit by recapturing some of the old vigor, and by improving on their methods of covering the territory. Dorothea Brande puts it thus: "All that is necessary to break the spell of inertia and frustration is this: Act as if it were impossible to fail. That is the talisman, the formula, the command of right-about-face which turns us from failure towards success."

Then let us not live in the past—whether our past be one of success or apparent failure. Neither should we dread the future, but face it expectantly.

> **Great works are performed not by strength but by perseverance.** —**Samuel Johnson**

My son, Timmy, has been selling since he was four. At this point that amounts to about one half of his young life. And he keeps improving.

This fellow begins during the pre-approach to decide just how much he can get from Dad. Next he sells himself by telling me that I am, beyond doubt, the strongest man on the block. This he shares with me while seated lovingly on my lap with his arms around Dad's neck. Then comes the pitch. "Dad," he might begin, "next week you will be going out of town; right? And you haven't bought me a gift for a while; right? And I *have* been a pretty good boy; right?" (Notice how he keeps me saying yes.)

Tim has learned the secret of asking for the order. Yes, he has learned this above all else. Talk about a guy being persistent. He asks for the order early and often. He reminds me several times before I even leave town. "Dad, what are you going to get me while you are out of town next week?" (Notice that this does not call for a yes or no answer.) This goes on rather consistently up to and including the day of my trip. On my return home, Timmy meets me at the car. Before I can even unload the luggage, he asks again for the order. "Well, Dad, did you remember to bring my present?"

Every salesman could take lessons from children. The only thing we need to do is dress up the children's presentations and make them a little more mature. Actually, there are few innovations in genuine selling. Most sales are neither sensational nor dramatic. Good sales are closed only after the proper mixture of inspiration and perspiration has been applied.

\* \* \*

Selling, relatively speaking, is still in its infancy. Be proud that you are a part of this great field of endeavor. The words of Charles F. Kettering are especially applicable to selling. "We are just at the beginning of progress in every field of human endeavor."